There Once Was A Dog Named Blue

Sue Ellen Lee

AuthorHouse™
1663 Liberty Drive
Bloomington, IN 47403
www.authorhouse.com
Phone: 1 (800) 839-8640

Published by AuthorHouse 08/03/2016

ISBN: 978-1-5246-1720-2 (sc)
ISBN: 978-1-5246-1721-9 (e)

Library of Congress Control Number: 2016910815

Print information available on the last page.

*Any people depicted in stock imagery provided by Thinkstock are models,
and such images are being used for illustrative purposes only.
Certain stock imagery © Thinkstock.*

This book is printed on acid-free paper.

*Because of the dynamic nature of the Internet, any web addresses or links contained in this book may have changed
since publication and may no longer be valid. The views expressed in this work are solely those of the author and do not
necessarily reflect the views of the publisher, and the publisher hereby disclaims any responsibility for them.*

authorHOUSE®

THERE
Once
WAS A
DOG
NAMED
BLUE

SUE ELLEN LEE

Dedication Page

This book is dedicated to Eunice H. Jones.

She came into my life and Blue's.

She shared many things with us:

Her enthusiasm, her caregiving,

Her love of life, her sense of humor,

Her French toast, her swimming pool,

Her family, and her baby-dog Sophia Grace.

FINE!!!

Acknowledgement

This book would never have been written without the hard work of Fran Warren. She worked at the Northumberland Animal Shelter for many years. It was her idea. She introduced me to Blue Boy and encouraged me to take him home. She thought it was fate that brought us together. Fran encouraged people to take a chance to save a life. Please go to a shelter and change your life.

My rescue dog rescued me.

There once was a dog named Blue.
This is what he liked to do!
Hello! My name is Sue Ellen and I want to tell you about my
best friend Blue Boy.

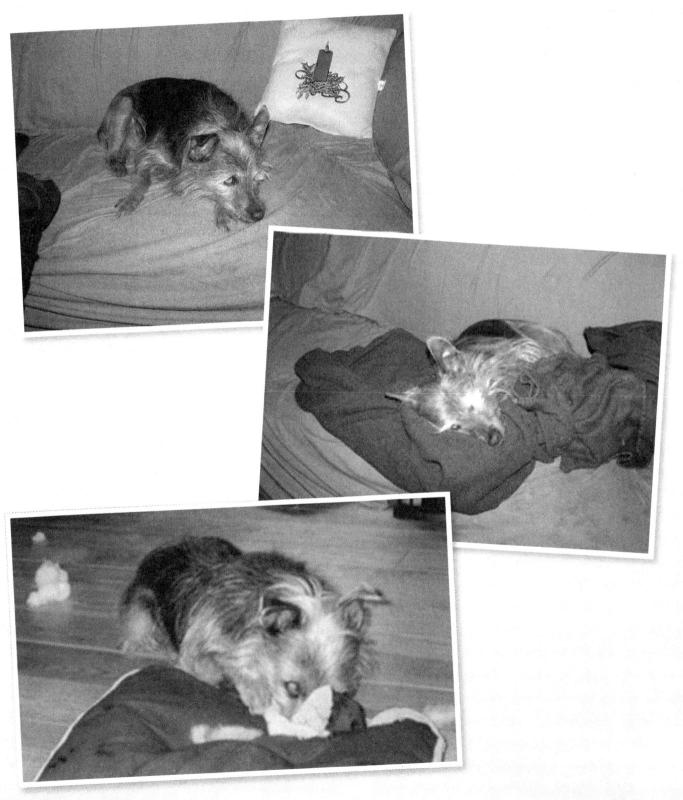

I live in a little town in the Northern Neck of Virginia called Weems. This is a very historic part of the country. Life is pretty calm here. I used to live in the city. This is better.

Most people here are fishermen or farmers.

The first thing I should tell you is I have to use a wheelchair because I cannot walk. I have a disease called muscular dystrophy. I have a car with a ramp and hand controls so I can still drive.

It was December of 2004. I was bored and driving around town Christmas shopping. Somehow I ended up at the Northumberland Animal Shelter. That day changed my life forever.

A very nice lady named Fran helped me. She brought out a little scruffy, dirty dog. She said someone brought him in on Christmas day. He had been walking around alone, all cold and hungry in a town named Lottsburg. He weighed about 15 pounds. He had beautiful blue eyes and he was blind. He seemed scared. I was worried I wouldn't be able to handle a blind dog. So I went home to think about it.

This is my house.

I left that day thinking about that little dog and came back two times to see him. He had already stolen my heart. I asked Fran to clean him up and cut his toenails. I named him Blue Boy because of his beautiful eyes.

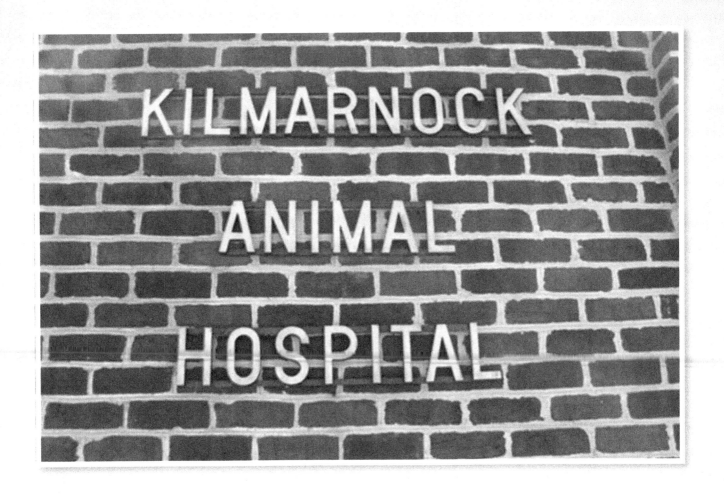

January 5, 2005, I brought him home. I took him to the vet to be checked out. The vet told me he was a cross between a Yorkshire terrier and a Chinese crested and he was very healthy. This is where our story begins. For ten years we have never been apart. We are growing old together.

I have never run over him. He seems to sense where I am. I think he knows my smell. He may also hear the engine on my wheelchair. He walks beside me or behind me. Sometimes he sits in my lap and rides.

For many years in the summer I have worked at a summer camp in Pennsylvania named Golden Slipper Camp. Blue Boy comes with me. One night we pretend that it is Halloween. The kids all dress up and collect candy. Blue Boy has several costumes. One is a cow and one is a Harley Davidson hat.

While we were at camp one summer Blue's left eye started to swell. It looked like it was going to pop out of his head. We went to the vet. The doctor told us that the pressure was probably giving Blue headaches. She operated and removed his eye. He had to wear a cone on his head so he would not touch his face. He looked pretty silly.

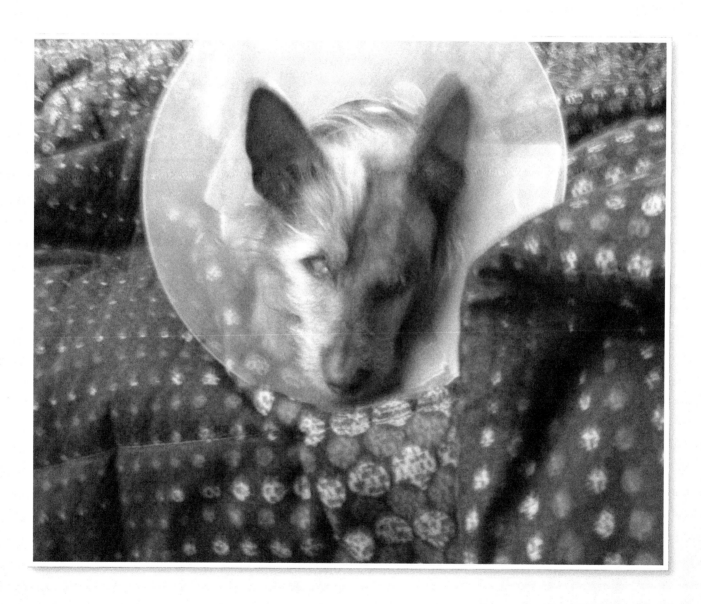

I wheel around all day checking up on everyone. Blue follows me everywhere I go. He does not wear a leash. All the kids love to pet him. He loves it, too.

He learned to sit in one meal. Either he's pretty smart or he learned it before I got him. We play together all the time. He loves to rip up magazines. His favorite food is chicken. He also loves rice with soy sauce.

But his absolute favorite thing to do is sleep.

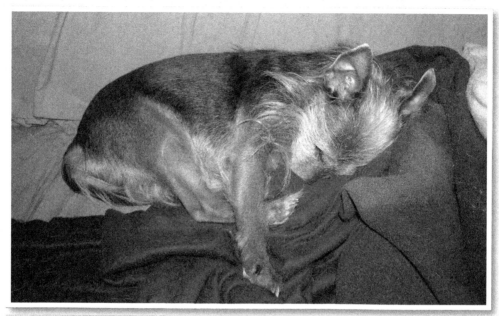

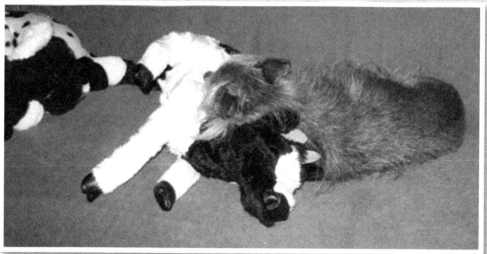

He follows me all over the place. We go pick up the mail every day at three o'clock. One night when we were outside, and he did not have his leash on, he ran off. I was terrified. I went to get a flashlight. I had no idea where he had gone. Blue was calmly waiting for me when I got to the mailbox.

He loves everybody he meets. People that is. He's not too crazy about other dogs.

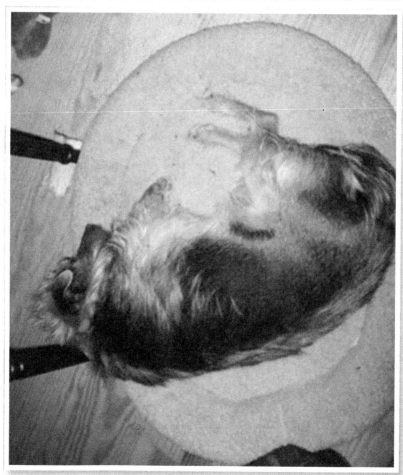

It just goes to show, that when you least expect it, wonderful things can happen. Any day! Blue is my very best friend. He has never been alone, cold or hungry again. Neither have I. Blue Boy saved my life. I like to think I saved his, too.

CPSIA information can be obtained at www.ICGtesting.com
Printed in the USA
BVOW05s0000190816

459490BV00004B/4/P